Think-Alongs™
Comprehending As You Read
Level F

Steck-Vaughn

Program Authors

Senior Author
Roger Farr

Co-Authors
Jennifer Conner
Elizabeth Haydel
Bruce Tone
Beth Greene
Tanja Bisesi
Cheryl Gilliland

STECK-VAUGHN
COMPANY

A Division of Harcourt Brace & Company

www.steck-vaughn.com

Acknowledgments

Editorial Director	Diane Schnell
Project Editor	Anne Souby
Associate Director of Design	Cynthia Ellis
Design Manager	Ted Krause
Production and Design	Julia Miracle-Hagaman
Photo Editor	Claudette Landry
Product Manager	Patricia Colacino
Cover Design	Ted Krause
Cover Sculpture	Lonnie Springer
Cover Production	Alan Klemp

Think-Alongs™ is a trademark of Steck-Vaughn Company.

ISBN 0-7398-0088-4

1 2 3 4 5 6 7 8 9   PO   03 02 01 00 99

Contents

Story Elements

Read the selection below. As you read, think about what the story is about (theme), where it takes place (setting), who is in it (characters), and what happens (plot).

As Deng looked out the window of his new apartment, nothing seemed familiar. He longed for his home across the ocean—for the chatter of people among the food carts, for the smell of the warm moist air. But he knew that he could never go back to that place or time.

Deng and his sister Lin had been in America for only a few weeks. Lin went out early that morning to work at the fish market. Deng put on his new winter coat and boots, walked down the long stairway, and stepped out onto the city sidewalk. He turned north into the wind and pushed his way through the snow. His mittenless hands ached as he held them deep down in his coat pockets.

Deng was so deep in thought that he almost walked past Mr. Park's tailor shop. Mr. Park had come to America more than thirty years ago and had built a very successful business. As Deng walked into the cozy shop, he hoped this would be the beginning of a successful life of his own.

As you read, you probably thought about the elements of the story. Check the boxes next to the ideas you had as you read.

This selection made me wonder if Deng would feel homesick for a long time.

I thought

☐ it would be scary to be alone in a new country.

☐ they must not have needed coats and mittens where they lived before.

☐ Deng will get a job with Mr. Park.

What else did you think about while you read?

_____

_____

_____

_____

Read and Think

- Read the selections that follow.
- Stop at each box and answer the question.
- Remember to think about what the story is about, where it takes place, who the characters are, and what happens.

THE WISE OLD WOMAN

Adapted by Yoshiko Uchida

Let's Read

This selection is a folktale about a lord, or ruler, in Japan who did not realize how important the old people in his village were. Read the selection to see how an old woman saves the village.

It is told that many long years ago, there lived an arrogant and cruel young lord. He ruled over a small village in the western hills of Japan.

"I have no use for old people in my village," he said haughtily. "They are neither useful nor able to work for a living. I therefore decree that anyone over seventy-one must be banished from the village and left in the mountains to die."

1   What kind of person do you think the lord is?

Shellfish

"What a terrible decree! What a cruel and unreasonable lord we have," the people of the village whispered. But the lord fearfully punished anyone who disobeyed him. So villagers who turned seventy-one were tearfully carried into the mountains, never to return.

Gradually, there were fewer and fewer old people in the village and soon they disappeared altogether. The young lord was pleased.

"What a fine village of young, healthy and hardworking people I have," he bragged. "Soon it will be the finest village in all Japan."

Now there lived in this village a kind young farmer and his aged mother. They were poor, but the farmer was good to his mother. The two of them lived happily together. However, as the years went by, the mother grew older, and before long she reached the terrible age of seventy-one.

"If only I could somehow deceive the cruel lord," the farmer thought. But there were records in the village books. Everyone knew that his mother had turned seventy-one.

Each day the son put off telling his mother that he must take her into the mountains to die, but the people of the village began to talk. The farmer knew that if he did not take his mother away soon, the lord would send his soldiers and throw them both into a dark dungeon to die.

"Mother—" he would begin, as he tried to tell her what he must do, but he could not go on.

Then one day the mother herself spoke of the lord's decree. "Well, my son," she said, "the time has come for you to take me to the mountains. We must hurry before the lord sends his soldiers for you." And she did not seem worried at all that she must go to the mountains to die.

2   What kind of person do you think the farmer is?

arely mine

"Forgive me, dear mother, for what I must do," the farmer said sadly, and the next morning he lifted his mother to his shoulders and set off on the steep path toward the mountains. Up and up he climbed, until the trees clustered close and the path was gone. There was no longer even the sound of birds, and they heard only the soft wail of the wind in the trees. The son walked slowly, for he could not bear to think of leaving his old mother in the mountains. On and on he climbed, not wanting to stop and leave her behind. Soon, he heard his mother breaking off small twigs from the trees that they passed.

"Mother, what are you doing?" he asked.

"Do not worry, my son," she answered gently. "I am just marking the way so you will not get lost returning to the village."

The son stopped. "Even now you are thinking of me?" he asked, wonderingly.

The mother nodded. "Of course, my son," she replied. "You will always be in my thoughts. How could it be otherwise?"

At that, the young farmer could bear it no longer. "Mother, I cannot leave you in the mountains to die all alone," he said. "We are going home. No matter what the lord does to punish me, I will never desert you again."

So they waited until the sun had set and a lone star crept into the silent sky. Then in the dark shadows of night, the farmer carried his mother down the hill and they returned quietly to their little house. The farmer dug a deep hole in the floor of his kitchen and made a small room where he could hide his mother. From that day, she spent all her time in the secret room and the farmer carried meals to her there. The rest of the time, he was careful to work in the fields and act as though he lived alone. In this way, for almost two years, he kept his mother safely hidden. No one in the village knew that she was there.

3 What do you think about the farmer's plan to save his mother?

good but somone mite no

Then one day there was a terrible commotion among the villagers. Lord Higa of the town beyond the hills threatened to take over their village and make it his own.

"Only one thing can spare you," Lord Higa announced. "Bring me a box containing one thousand ropes of ash and I will spare your village."

The cruel young lord quickly gathered together all the wise men of his village. "You are men of wisdom," he said. "Surely you can tell me how to meet Lord Higa's demands so our village can be spared."

But the wise men shook their heads. "It is impossible to make even one rope of ash, sire," they answered. "How can we ever make one thousand?"

"Fools!" the lord cried angrily. "What good is your wisdom if you cannot help me now?"

And he posted a notice in the village square offering a great reward of gold to any villager who could help him save their village.

But all the people in the village whispered, "Surely, it is an impossible thing, for ash crumbles at the touch of the finger. How could anyone ever make a rope of ash?" They shook their heads and sighed, "Alas, alas, we must be taken over by yet another cruel lord."

The young farmer, too, supposed that this must be. He wondered what would happen to his mother if a new lord even more terrible than their own came to rule over them.

When his mother saw the troubled look on his face, she asked, "Why are you so worried, my son?"

So the farmer told her of the impossible task ordered by Lord Higa if the village was to be spared, but his mother did not seem troubled at all. Instead she laughed softly and said, "Why, that is not such an impossible task. All one has to do is soak ordinary rope in salt water and dry it well. When it is burned, it will hold its shape and there is your rope of ash! Tell the villagers to hurry and find one thousand pieces of rope."

The farmer shook his head in amazement. "Mother, you are wonderfully wise," he said. He rushed to tell the young lord what he must do.

4 What do you think of the mother for telling the son how to save the village?

good

"You are wiser than all the wise men of the village," the lord said when he heard the farmer's solution. He rewarded him with many pieces of gold. The thousand ropes of ash were quickly made and the village was spared.

In a few days, however, there was another great commotion in the village as Lord Higa sent another threat. This time he sent a log with a small hole that curved and bent seven times through its length. He ordered that a single piece of silk thread be threaded through the hole. "If you cannot perform this task," the lord threatened, "I shall come to take over your village."

The young lord hurried once more to his wise men, but they all shook their heads in bewilderment. "A needle cannot bend its way through such curves," they moaned. "Again we are faced with an impossible task."

"And again you are stupid fools!" the lord said, stamping his foot impatiently. He then posted a second notice in the village square asking the villagers for their help.

Once more the young farmer hurried with the problem to his mother in her secret room.

"Why, that is not so difficult," his mother said with a quick smile. "Put some sugar at one end of the hole. Then, tie an ant to a piece of silk thread and put it in at the other end. He will weave his way in and out of the curves to get to the sugar and he will take the silk thread with him."

"Mother, you are remarkable!" the son cried, and he hurried off to the lord with the solution to the second problem.

Once more the lord commended the young farmer and rewarded him with many pieces of gold. "You are a brilliant man. You have saved our village again," he said gratefully.

But the lord's troubles were not over even then, for a few days later Lord Higa sent still another task. "This time you will undoubtedly fail and then I shall take over your village," he threatened. "Bring me a drum that sounds without being beaten."

"But that is not possible," sighed the people of the village. "How can anyone make a drum sound without beating it?"

This time the wise men held their heads in their hands and moaned, "It is hopeless. It is hopeless. This time Lord Higa will defeat us all."

The young farmer hurried home breathlessly. "Mother, Mother, we must solve another terrible problem or Lord Higa will take over our village!" And he quickly told his mother about the impossible drum.

His mother, however, smiled and answered, "Why, this is the easiest of them all. Make a drum with sides of paper and put a bumblebee inside. As it tries to escape, it will buzz and beat itself against the paper and you will have a drum that sounds without being beaten."

The young farmer was amazed at his mother's wisdom. "You are far wiser than any of the wise men of the village," he said. He hurried to tell the young lord how to complete Lord Higa's third task.

When the lord heard the answer, he was greatly impressed. "Surely a young man like you cannot be wiser than all my wise men," he said. "Tell me honestly, who has helped you solve all these difficult problems?"

5 What do you think the farmer will do now?

I don't no

The young farmer could not lie. "My lord," he began slowly, "for the past two years I have broken the law of the land. I have kept my aged mother hidden beneath the floor of my house. It is she who solved each of your problems and saved the village from Lord Higa."

He trembled as he spoke, for he feared the lord's displeasure and rage. Surely now the soldiers would be called to throw him into the dark dungeon. But when he glanced fearfully at the lord, he saw that the young ruler was not angry at all. Instead, he was silent and thoughtful. At last the lord realized how much wisdom and knowledge old people possess.

"I have been very wrong," he said finally. "And I must ask the forgiveness of your mother and of all my people. Never again will I order that the old people of our village be sent to the mountains to die. Rather, they will be treated with the respect and honor they deserve and share with us the wisdom of their years."

And so it was. From that day, the villagers were no longer forced to leave their parents in the mountains. The village became once more a happy, cheerful place in which to live. The terrible Lord Higa stopped sending his impossible tasks and no longer threatened to take over the village, for he too was impressed. "Even in such a small village there is much wisdom," he declared, "and its people should be allowed to live in peace."

And that is exactly what the farmer and his mother and all the people of the village did for all the years thereafter.

6   What lesson does this story teach?

Time to Write!

In this folktale, as in many folktales, the main characters had to solve problems. Folktales also teach a lesson.

- For this activity, you will write a folktale that presents a problem to be solved and a lesson to be learned.

Prewriting

First, complete the story summary below.

Characters	Setting (Time and Place)

Plot (Problem and Solution)	Theme (Lesson)

Writing

Now, use another sheet of paper to write your folktale.

The Kicking Cow

By Barbara Bartholomew

This selection is about a boy who nervously takes over one of the farm chores his father used to do—milking the family's cow. Read the selection to find out what happens when he milks Emily, the cow.

When they came back to the farm, everything was the same, except that Papa wasn't there anymore.

Jack lingered in the car, watching his mother and sisters head toward the closed-up house. For the last four weeks they'd stayed with Aunt Elizabeth's family, and while they'd been gone, the world had moved from winter into spring.

He jumped down from the running board to walk through scratchy, ankle-deep weeds, past a scattering of chickens, to the place back of the barn where Emily, the cow, and Bob, their old horse, grazed on sparse, sickly looking grass.

Emily only stared solemnly, but Bob neighed a welcome and trotted up to have his soft nose rubbed and his gray dappled neck stroked.

Jack buried his face in the old horse's bristly mane, and for a minute he seemed to hear Papa calling.

"Jackie, what are you doing lallygagging around when there's chores to be done!" Even while scolding, his voice was full of cheerful good humor.

Papa was like that. No matter how hard things got, and with the drought lately that had been plenty hard, he always seemed to think life was meant to be fun.

Jack scrubbed the tears from his face with horsehair, trying not to think about Papa because it hurt too much.

"No lallygagging," he whispered sternly to himself.

1 What kind of person do you think Jack is?

Since they'd been gone all those weeks, the work had piled up. The fence needed mending, and shingles were missing on the roof of the barn. The potatoes needed hoeing, and it was time for cotton and the garden to be planted. They had more than enough to keep them busy: he, Mama, Dorrie, and Janet. Keeping busy would be the best thing. That way he wouldn't always be hearing Papa's deep voice ringing in his ears.

"Jackie," his younger sister called. "Where are you, Jackie?"

His first thought was to hide so she couldn't find him. Lately Dorrie seemed always just behind him, tagging along like his shadow.

"Jackie!" Her voice was louder now, shrill and whiny.

"Down here. In the pasture."

She came running around the barn, a skinny little seven-year-old with sticklike legs, dressed in an ugly faded yellow dress. Her thin, freckled face lighted at the sight of him. "I've been looking all over for you."

He gave old Bob a final pat. "Been right here all the time."

"Mrs. Bagby cleaned up for us and left supper on the stove. Mama says to come and eat while it's still hot."

Yellow jackets buzzed and hummed in the afternoon sun, but none made any threatening sweeps toward him or Dorrie as they strolled back toward the house. The heavy scent of roses blooming on the bush by the back step mixed with the sneezy breath of dust stirred by their footsteps.

 2 How is Jack's home like your home?

Supper was hot, fresh-baked corn bread, homemade pickles, and cold, sweet milk. They crumbled the bread into the milk and spooned up the warm, fragrant mixture, varying its blandness with bites of crunchy dill pickle.

After supper, they left Dorrie to wash the dishes while the rest of them scattered outside to do the evening chores. Sixteen-year-old Janet went to feed the chickens and gather eggs, and Jack followed Mama to the barn, where she took the milking bucket from a hook on the wall.

"I'll do that."

She stared at him. Milking used to be Papa's job. Mama had taken to doing it in the weeks while he was sick.

Finally she nodded, handing him the bucket. "Be careful you don't get kicked."

Emily was an easy milker and gave plentiful amounts, rich with cream. But her one fault was that she liked to kick. Last winter Papa had limped around for weeks, recovering from a blow delivered by one of her sharp hoofs.

 3 What do you think will happen when Jack milks the cow?

Jack regarded Emily with healthy respect and even a measure of fear. He'd demanded to be allowed to do the milking because he was afraid. He had to face up to that fear and make it go away.

He went into the barn for hay, fed a little to Bob first, then left him munching while he attended to Emily.

By the time Emily was busy eating her hay, he'd fetched the three-legged wooden stool from the barn. He placed the bucket under Emily's udder and sat on the stool up close to her warm side. She loomed like a mountain above him, and her tail, swishing at flies, twitched into his face, making his cheek sting.

He grasped a teat in each hand and began to twist and squeeze to make the milk come out. His work produced steady streams that poured into the metal bucket with a satisfactory clatter.

When the bucket was nearly half full, he began to feel better about himself, almost forgetting what Emily might do next.

Her fly-chasing tail swished again, but this time Jack managed to duck without missing a beat in his milking.

"We're going to get along fine, Emily," he gloated. "Just fine."

Emily's back leg flashed out, sending the bucket flying and tumbling Jack and the stool to the hard, bare ground.

 4 How does Jack feel now about milking Emily?

For an instant he felt as though the breath had been knocked out of him. Then he drew in air and released it again in a long, shaky sigh.

He was twelve, he reminded himself of that. Plenty old enough to deal with a muley old cow.

Milk spilled from the overturned bucket, seeping quickly into the ground. Even before taking stock of his own injuries, even before trying to sit up, Jack grabbed the bucket and righted it.

Only a few drops remained, clinging to the bottom and sides. Feeling sick, Jack got to his feet.

All that milk—milk to drink and milk to feed the calf, milk for butter and cream—gone. He hated the thought of having to tell Mama.

His left leg ached, and he'd scraped an elbow, but worse was the fear that Emily's hoof might flash out at him again any minute. He thought of calling Mama and asking her to finish the milking, but was immediately ashamed.

5   Why was Jack ashamed?

He approached Emily warily. The Jersey crunched her hay calmly, seeming unaware of the commotion she'd caused. Or maybe she just didn't care.

"Easy, Emily," Jack spoke soothingly. Though the cow didn't seem in need of calming, his own jangled nerves sure did.

His mouth dry and his muscles tight, he sat again on the little stool. "Easy, Emily."

Her tail swished against the side of his face, making him jump just a little. He glanced around, glad no one was there to witness his fear.

" 'Bout finished down there, Jackie?" Mama's voice called from somewhere up near the house.

"Be right there, Mama," he called back.

By the time he rose from the stool, gratified that he'd gotten through the rest of the milking without another kick, the bucket was nearly half full again.

Janet was slopping the hogs in a nearby pen as he got ready to feed the calf.

She glanced into the bucket. "Not much milk tonight."

He poured milk into the calf's feeding bucket, keeping back only a small amount for house use. The calf had to be fed her milk first. They got what was left.

"Emily kicked the bucket over. Spilled more than half the milk."

"She used to kick Papa once in a while," said Janet. "And sometimes the milk got spilled."

6   What is Janet's opinion of her brother?

It was hard to imagine, but maybe even Papa had been a little scared of being kicked. But he'd just kept on, going out to milk Emily every night.

And maybe now Mama and Dorrie and Janet were scared sometimes, not liking the idea of having to go on without Papa any more than he did. But they all had to keep on.

The calf was finished drinking. "Race you to the house," he said to Janet.

7 What is the theme of this story?

Time to Write!

Write a description of a character that you think is special. The person could be someone you know or a character from a book, film, or a TV program. Tell how the character looks, sounds, and acts.

• In this activity, you will write a character sketch.

Prewriting

First, answer the questions below.

What is the character's name? _____

What is special about the character? _____

_____

_____

How did the character look, sound, or act? _____

_____

_____

Why did you choose this character?_____

_____

_____

Writing

Now, use another sheet of paper to write a descriptive sketch about the character.

Morning Girl

By Michael Dorris

Let's Read

This selection is a chapter from a book telling the story of a girl, Morning Girl, her younger brother, Star Boy, and their family. Read the selection to find out about a special time in their lives.

[Note: This story takes place on an island in the Bahamas in the year 1492. The people on the island have just survived a violent storm. This chapter is told from Morning Girl's point of view.]

No one had died. The storm had damaged nothing that could not be built again. Who needed a roof when the sun shone so friendly or when the stars glowed overhead, watching our sleep? The wind had cleared a new path across the island, wide and open, and all along it, the old was suddenly new, made clean, set out in a different way.

Father, Mother, and I followed the wind's trail to find Star Boy tucked in the arms of the tree where the new sister stayed with Grandfather. When we told Grandmother what had happened, how my brother had been caught and protected, her smile took over her whole face, squeezing shut her small, dark eyes and pushing her chin into her chest when she bowed her head. She told us that Grandfather had once saved Father, too, long ago, from a shark—which was how he got his old man's name, Fast Arms.

1 What do you think has happened on the island?

People from other families couldn't remain at their homes. "Our houses didn't stay put," they joked when they passed us. "Why should we?"

How easy it was, that first long day, to gather what we needed. The palms were already spread on the ground, perfect for thatch. Coconuts lay where they had fallen, and even, in some unexpected places—large puddles or places where the ponds had spilled over their banks—silver fish carried from the sea could amazingly be found.

2 What are you thinking about now?

The high tides had left the beach flat and smooth, and beyond, the water was tipped with gold where the sun patted the rippling waves.

Of course, there was much work to be done . . . but not on the first day, Father decided, and not on the second, either. Instead, he said this was a chance to be happy together, to dance and make music on hollow logs, to watch ball games, to sing good-bye to the wind, and to share the food that had been presented to us as its apology. It was the time for each person to tell a story, to act it out while the rest of us held our heads in fear or covered our mouths when the laughter grew too strong to contain.

3   What do you think they are going to tell stories about?

Mother found dry sticks and poured fire from her pot, then roasted some sweet potatoes in a pit she dug in the ground. Star Boy and I searched among the trees, looking under branches and drooping leaves to find fruit that had not burst. I tried not to count or notice that I found three more than he did. After all, my arms were long, and, anyway, I knew his story would be better than mine.

A large crowd of grandparents, adults, children, and babies had already assembled near The Digging Stick, the place where the land rocks curve into the ocean. I was shy at first because of seeing so many people at once—that almost never happened except when there was a marriage or when someone died. Another thing was different, too, though for a while I couldn't place what it was. Then I knew! The wind had swept away most of the tiny bugs, the ones that were all mouth, the ones that ate and ate and were never full. Usually, when the air was still, people had to burn smudge fires or rub ashes and soot on their bodies to discourage the appetites of those bugs. At such times, we turned into a gray people, except for our hair and lips and eyes. But today we were bright as wet shells, each person painted and decorated differently. Some wore flattened gold leaves in their earlobes, some placed hibiscus blooms in their hair or hung long necklaces of shells around their necks.

 4   What are you thinking about now?

Wherever I looked there was food, food, food—all the secret recipes from each family there to taste, more food than I had ever seen.

Star Boy, probably because he was so sure his adventure would be admired, was not timid. He raced ahead of us with his hands open and took some wonderful thing to eat from each mat he passed.

I didn't think much of this—I was used to my brother being a child, and he was simply behaving the way a child behaves, no worse than that. I remembered when I could run free, not worrying that I might appear foolish, and there was a part of me that wished I could join Star Boy now: do whatever I wanted with no aunt's or uncle's eyes to correct me or to embarrass Mother by staring at me too hard. I had received those looks only once, and that had been too much, more than enough to remind me that though I had not yet become a woman, I was no longer a child.

 5 What do you think of Star Boy's behavior?

And then, as I watched, I realized that Star Boy was not a child anymore, either, that he had become too old for such play in public, and I saw all around him those terrible looks, pointed at him.

Now he'll learn, I thought, with more rightness than kindness.

But Star Boy didn't notice. His eyes were full of the surprise of not blowing away, too proud, too excited, too—

A big boy, Never Cry, spoke the word I was thinking:

"Hungry!" Never Cry called to my brother. "You're well named."

A few people laughed, and didn't even cover their mouths. Father touched Mother's arm just above her elbow. Her lips pressed together, and I knew how she felt: how could Star Boy be wrong on so fine a day?

"I'm not Hungry anymore," my brother told Never Cry, loud enough for all to hear. He was so pleased with himself, that he hadn't understood. "I'm Star Boy now, because—"

 6   What are you thinking about now?

My uncle, Sharp Tooth, interrupted. "The wind still must be flowing," he said to Father. "It mixes words and meanings. I thought I heard your little Hungry say he had a grown boy's name, but look, he's the same as ever, the same as he has always been."

My brother stopped where he was. His hands were filled with food he couldn't drop and waste. There was fresh honey smeared on his chin. He closed his eyes, then opened them. He looked at me.

I don't know how long we stood that way, but it was as if just the two of us were there. I was aware of the sounds of babies, of waves, of the birds as they flapped their wings above the food, but I heard them through deep water. Star Boy and I reached across the space between us, we made a fishing line with our eyes and each pulled the other to the center.

"Food!" I sang, loud as my voice would reach. "Food! I'm so hungry I can't wait any longer to eat!"

I ran through the crowd, following the path my brother had broken, sampling and reaching like the youngest child, filling my mouth until I couldn't talk, until I reached Star Boy.

7 Why do you think Morning Girl did what her brother did?

I was so quiet I could hear my mouth chewing.

"Let us eat!" called Father, behind me. "This family is hungry. We forgot food while we searched for our son, Star Boy, who watches over us during the night. Now our stomachs rule our brains."

I turned and glanced up quickly, watched as Father took a fruit in each hand and lifted them to his face. The juice ran down his chest as he took bite after bite.

"Perhaps you are not hungry, little Sharp Tooth," my mother said to her brother. "Perhaps you slept when the wind passed over, or perhaps you are not hungry because you are already too heavy for even a hurricane to lift. But me, I am hungry."

"Me, too," growled the voice of Grandmother, off to the side of where I stood staring at the ground before my feet.

"And me," said our neighbor I Swam Too Far, who had helped us search for Star Boy.

 8   What are you thinking about now?

The tide had changed, and people began to look to my uncle instead of at my brother and me. For a moment, his face grew full of the anger that comes from being wrong, but then, swift as yesterday's rain had departed, he set it free.

"Star Boy," Sharp Tooth called. "Bring me some sweet lemon. Find me a coconut to drink. Let me be the first to know your story so that I can introduce my nephew by his proper name when you tell everyone else what happened."

Names are strange and special gifts. There are names you give to yourself and names you show to the world, names that stay for a short while and names that remain with you forever, names that come from things you do and names that you receive as presents from other people. No one would forget that my brother had once been Hungry, but today they would listen for who he had become. And Star Boy, too, would remember that he was now older, that he could no longer behave as a child. If your name is true, it is who you are.

I swallowed the last of the food in my mouth and lifted my eyes. Star Boy had not moved.

"It's all right," I whispered to him. "Go."

And he did, finally, but not before he spoke so that only I could hear, not before he had called me the name he would always afterward use when we were alone together, not before he had said, so softly, "The One Who Stands Beside."

9   Why are names so important to the island people?

Time to Write!

Think about an event that made you realize that you were not a child anymore. For example, it could be the first time you went to a fancy restaurant or you were asked to take care of a sibling by yourself.

• For this activity, you will write a story about a special event that made you realize you were no longer a child.

Prewriting

First, use the boxes below to help you organize your thoughts.

Event

Where it was	Who was there

What happened	How you felt

Writing

Now, use another sheet of paper to write your story.

Problems and Solutions

You may have read *The Midnight Fox* by Betsy Byars. Tom, the boy in the story, faces a problem. Read about Tom's problem and think about the possible solutions.

Tom is spending the summer with Aunt Millie and Uncle Fred at their farm. During his stay Tom discovers a black fox and her cub in the woods and is awed by the intelligence, beauty, and wonder of the "midnight fox." However, the fox has been stealing turkeys and eggs from Aunt Millie's coop. Uncle Fred captures the baby fox from the fox's den. He knows the mother fox will come looking for her cub, and he intends to shoot the fox so she won't steal any more of Aunt Millie's turkeys or turkey eggs.

That night there is a thunderstorm, and Uncle Fred goes to bed without having shot the fox. Tom tosses and turns in bed thinking about what to do. He doesn't want the midnight fox to be killed, but he knows that the fox may go on killing Aunt Millie's turkeys. He thinks about getting up in the middle of the night and opening the cage so the fox cub can escape, but he worries about what Aunt Millie and Uncle Fred will think. He doesn't want the midnight fox and her cub to be killed, but . . .

What should Tom do? Should he stand by while Uncle Fred shoots the midnight fox? Should he free the fox cub from the cage? How will he face Uncle Fred and Aunt Millie if he lets the cub get away? Check what Tom might consider in solving his problem:

I think Tom should find a way to keep the fox from getting the turkeys.

☐ how Tom will feel if the fox and her cub are killed

☐ what Tom will say to Uncle Fred and Aunt Millie if he lets the fox cub escape

☐ what will happen to the turkeys if the midnight fox is not killed

What would you do if you were Tom?

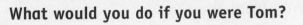

_____

_____

_____

_____

Read and Think

- Read the selections that follow.
- Stop at each box and answer the question.
- Think about the problems and solutions as you read. Think about what you might do if you were faced with these problems.

Seed Travel

By Ann Ackroyd

Let's Read

This selection is about how seeds become travelers. Read the selection to learn why seeds need to travel and the many different ways that they travel.

We like to think only humans use rockets, helicopters, parachutes, and gliders, but that's not true. Other travelers used such methods long before we did. These travelers are seeds! But why would a seed need to travel?

Seeds need to get away from their parent plants. If they remain too close, young plants starve. Their bigger, stronger parents overshadow them, hogging sunlight and water. It's also a seed's job to claim new living space for its species.

Broom

1   What problem do seeds have?

Have you ever watched a toy rocket take off with a small explosion? The Mediterranean squirting cucumber behaves like a rocket—without the fire. The little cucumber fills with juice until it's so full, it bursts off its stalk. A trail of slime follows it as it shoots through the air. This slime contains the seeds.

Plants with pods launch their seeds using another kind of explosion. When broom seeds are ready, the sun warms one side of the pod and dries it. The other side remains in shadow and dries more slowly. The sides pull against each other until the pod splits, hurling the seeds away from the parent plant. A Brazilian tree called the monkey's dinner bell does the same. It pops so loudly, strangers think they are under attack. The seeds can travel 40 feet, so it's best not to be in the way.

2 What are some ways that seeds travel?

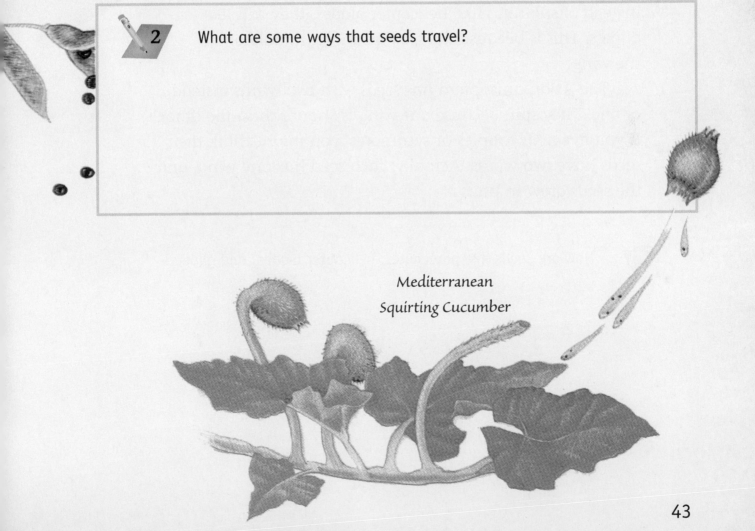

Mediterranean
Squirting Cucumber

43

Alsomitra

Anisoptera

Many seeds use parachutes. Think of dandelion puffs—they contain hundreds of tiny seeds, each with its own silky parachute for riding the wind. Milkweed seeds come in pods instead of blowballs. If you open a ripe milkweed pod, you will see a packaging miracle. Hundreds of seed heads overlap neatly, while their closed parachutes lie flat, resembling hair.

Some seeds have wings to help them glide away from their parent plants. The simplest designs have one wing. Have you ever seen pine seeds leave an open cone? If so, you know that each seed sits at the base of a paper-thin wing. As the seed falls, it whirls through the air like a helicopter blade. The seeds of the alsomitra, an Asian creeper, also have one wing, but instead of spinning like helicopter blades, they sail like gliders. This is because the seed sits in the middle of the wing.

The Asian anisoptera has seeds with two wings instead of one. They spin because one wing is shorter than the other. If you live near maples or sycamores, you might think their seeds have two wings. Actually, each seed has one wing, and the seeds grow in pairs.

 3 How are seeds like parachutes, helicopter blades, and gliders?

Coconut

Some seeds travel in water by floating. The coconut is one example. Air spaces between its outer shell and the hairy inner seed keep it from sinking. A sweet, milky liquid in the center nourishes the seed.

The sea bean provides its seeds with wooden cases that can stay afloat for a year. These seeds ride the Gulf Stream and sometimes land in Europe—4,000 miles away from their parents in the Caribbean.

Many seeds hitchhike. Some use hooks to grab an animal's fur or a person's clothing. The next time you pull cockleburs from your socks, remember that you are helping the burdock plant expand its territory.

Other hitchhiking seeds ride inside the animals that eat them. They do this by hiding in fruits like strawberries and raspberries. All such hitchhikers have the advantage of landing in a pile of fertilizer!

4 What are some other ways that seeds travel?

Cocklebur

Hickory

A number of plants use only one seed carrier. Oaks and hickories belong to this group. The armor around their seeds is so thick, only a squirrel can break it. However, a squirrel collects more acorns and hickory nuts than it can eat. It hides the extras to eat later. But the extras aren't always needed, and sometimes a squirrel forgets its hidden treasure. The uneaten seeds grow into new trees far from their parents.

Look around and see if you can find more seedy rockets, helicopters, parachutes, hitchhikers, and floaters. Or what about seeds that travel in other ways? Look at a poppy, for instance. It acts like a salt shaker, shaking out its seeds. Once you start noticing how seeds travel, you'll want to make your own list.

5 What was the problem and solution in this selection?

Time to Write!

You have learned about ways that seeds travel. Imagine how it would feel to travel as a seed. Choose a seed from the selection. Tell how it travels and what happens to it along the way.

- For this activity, you will write a description of your travels as a seed.

Prewriting

First, answer the following questions.

What seed will you choose?

_____

How do you travel?

_____

What does it feel like to travel this way?

_____

What problems might you run into when you travel?

_____

What do you like about traveling this way?

_____

What might you see as you travel?

_____

How do you feel at the end of your trip?

_____

Writing

Now, use another sheet of paper to write your story about yourself as a traveling seed.

Walking the Road to Freedom: A Story About Sojourner Truth

By Jeri Ferris

Let's Read

This selection is about Sojourner Truth, a woman who escaped slavery and then fought against slavery throughout her life. Read about the problems Sojourner Truth faced and how she solved those problems.

It was June 1, 1843, when Sojourner Truth walked out of New York City. She spent part of her twenty-five cents on a boat ride across the East River and then walked east along Long Island's sandy roads. That evening she knocked on a farmhouse door and asked for work in exchange for supper and a place to sleep. The farmer's kind wife wrote a letter for Sojourner to send to her daughters so they wouldn't worry.

Sojourner walked on and in a few days came to a religious camp meeting. There were tents and wagons and people spread out all over the hillside, talking and singing.

Sojourner stopped to do some talking and singing of her own. People gathered around, looking with curiosity at this very tall and very black woman with deep, wise eyes, dressed in a neat Quaker dress and a white shawl, with a white turban on her head. Sojourner told them about her life as a slave.

48

Then in her low voice, as rich and warm as dark maple syrup, she began to sing, "It was early in the morning, just at the break of day. . . ." Her astonished audience listened in awe and asked her to stay a few days so they could hear more.

 1 What problem did Sojourner talk and sing about?

As the summer passed, Sojourner became well-known at religious meetings in New York and Connecticut and Massachusetts. People told others to be sure to go and hear Sojourner Truth.

One evening while Sojourner was at a camp meeting in Massachusetts, a mob of young men appeared. They swarmed through the tents, overturning wagons and swinging bottles and sticks. Sojourner was as frightened as everybody else. She decided to help. She got up from her hiding place, smoothed her dress, walked to a small hill, and began to sing. The mob quickly surrounded her, leaving the rest of the camp alone and quiet under the full moon. Sojourner stood calm and unafraid in the midst of the mob, her voice soaring through the treetops, until the young men left the camp meeting in peace.

When all was quiet, Sojourner's friends came out from behind their tents. "You tamed that wild mob," they said, shaking their heads, "with just your voice."

 2 How did Sojourner solve the problem with the mob of young men?

That fall Sojourner traveled to Massachusetts to spend a day in Northampton, a community of people who believed that slavery was wrong and that all people were equal before God. Northampton was not a pretty place. Its large, untidy factory buildings were surrounded by bare, frozen meadows.

Men, women, and children worked side by side raising silkworms and making silk cloth. No one had time to cook properly or clean or do the laundry. Sojourner could do all these things, so she decided to stay and help for a while. As she worked, she had the children read passages to her from the Bible so she could memorize them.

It was in Northampton that, for the first time, Sojourner was introduced to people who were determined to stop slavery. She met people who were traveling all over New York and many other northern states to explain how and why slavery must end. She met William Lloyd Garrison and other abolitionists, people who were devoting their lives to the fight against slavery. And she met Frederick Douglass, a fiery young black man who had escaped from slavery in 1838. Sojourner listened eagerly to the talk about the antislavery meetings these men were holding, and she added their ideas to her own knowledge of slavery.

Sojourner found that the arguments over slavery were getting hotter. Congress passed a new and harsher fugitive slave law, which said that anyone who helped a slave escape could be put in prison. Although slavery was now prohibited in the northern states, a freed slave in the North could be dragged South if two white men swore that he or she was escaped property. Many northerners thought this was outrageous. More people began to listen to the antislavery speakers.

3 How did the slavery problem change?

The story of Frederick Douglass's life as a southern slave was published in 1845. But the story of a southern slave did not convince people in the North that slavery had to be stopped. Abolitionists thought the story of a *northern* slave—Sojourner Truth, for example—might do the job.

So Sojourner told the story of her life to a friend. In 1850 *The Narrative of Sojourner Truth: A Northern Slave* was published—a thin, brown paper-covered book with Sojourner's picture on the first page.

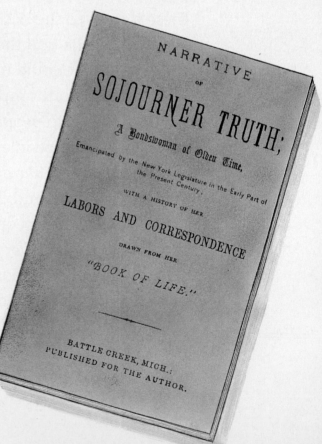

Sojourner filled her carpetbag with copies of her book and set off for antislavery meetings throughout the northern United States. At first she only listened to the other speakers, but one evening Mr. Garrison told the audience that Sojourner Truth would be the first speaker.

Sojourner knew that the next speaker would be Wendell Phillips, a well-known abolitionist, and she wondered what she could say to be different from him. What could she do to make people remember what she said? She decided to sing a new song she had made up about black men and women in slavery.

Sojourner walked confidently to the speakers' platform, dressed as always in plain Quaker style. In her strong, deep voice she began to sing, "I am pleading for my people, a poor down-trodden race, who dwell in freedom's boasted land with no abiding place. . . ."

After the meeting people crowded around Sojourner asking for copies of her "homemade" songs and for her book and for pictures (Sojourner called them "shadows") of herself.

She soon became one of the most powerful speakers in the antislavery fight and one of the few black women to speak to white audiences.

4 How did Sojourner work to solve the slavery problem?

Sojourner met many women—Amy Post, Lucretia Mott, and others—who raised money for the abolitionists, taught former slaves to read and write, and helped slaves escape on the Underground Railroad. (The Underground Railroad was not a railroad that ran underground. It was a network of safe houses where escaped slaves could hide on the long, dangerous journey to Canada, where they would be free.) From these women Sojourner learned about another fight. This one was for women's rights. In 1850 a woman could not vote or own property. Many of the men who opposed slavery, including Frederick Douglass, also spoke out for women's rights. After all, they agreed, when we see one injustice we see the other as well. Sojourner, being a woman, gladly joined the fight for women's rights too.

 5   What new problem did Sojourner begin to battle?

Some women did not welcome her. They feared that if women's rights got mixed up with the antislavery fight, both would fail. Sojourner soon proved them wrong.

In 1851 she attended the Women's Rights Convention in Akron, Ohio. As the meeting progressed, men in the audience began to ridicule the women for wanting to be treated as men's equals. "Women are weak," they shouted. "Weak in body and weak in mind. Women have to be taken care of by men."

Sojourner looked around. No one seemed to know what to do. She set her sunbonnet down and slowly stood up. "Don't let her speak," some of the women said loudly.

But chairwoman Frances Gage, who was trying to quiet the audience, smiled with relief. "Sojourner Truth," she announced.

Sojourner looked quietly at the scoffing crowd. Then she pointed to the man who had just spoken. "That man over there," she said in her powerful voice, "that man says that women need to be helped into carriages and lifted over ditches and have the best place everywhere. Nobody ever helps me into carriages or over mud puddles or gives me any best place! And ain't I a woman?"

Sojourner pushed up one sleeve. "Look at my arm! I have plowed and planted and gathered into barns, and no man could beat me! And ain't I a woman? I could work as much and eat as much as a man—when I could get it—and bear the lash as well! And ain't I a woman?"

The crowd sat in stunned silence, hardly daring to breathe. Sojourner finished and sat down on the steps again. Then the audience, women and men, wiped their eyes and applauded wildly. "You reached our hearts," one man called.

6 How did Sojourner try to convince people that women should have more rights?

Mrs. Gage wrote later, "She picked us up in her strong arms and carried us over the difficulties. She turned the tide in our favor. I have never in my life seen anything like her magical influence."

For two years Sojourner traveled throughout Ohio with a borrowed horse and buggy and 600 copies of her *Narrative*. She held her own meetings, and she spoke at every abolitionist and women's rights meeting within horse-trotting distance. She bounced over rutted roads and past hills covered with dark forests; she drove by log cabins and sturdy farmhouses. When she came to a town, she'd stop her horse in the middle of the street and begin to sing. That got people's attention. Then Sojourner would speak, and that kept people's attention.

Epilogue

On January 1, 1863, 20 years after Sojourner had started preaching and singing against slavery, President Lincoln signed the Emancipation Proclamation. This was what Sojourner had worked and prayed for. Her people were free.

7 What problem was solved by the Emancipation Proclamation?

Time to Write!

Sojourner Truth tried to solve problems. Think of someone you know or you have learned about who tried to solve a problem.

• For this activity, you will write an article about the person who tried to solve a problem.

Prewriting

First, answer the questions below.

What person are you going to write about?

_____

Why did you choose this person?

_____

What problem did the person try to solve?

_____

What caused the problem?

_____

_____

What did the person do to try to solve the problem?

_____

_____

Writing

Now, use another sheet of paper to write your article about a person who tried to solve a problem.

57

The following two selections tell about guide dogs for the blind. The first is about a girl who is legally blind and gets a dog to help her. The second is about a girl who trains a puppy to become a guide dog.

Where She Leads, I Will Follow

By Tiffany Medina

This selection is about a girl who is legally blind and her new guide dog. Read the selection to find out how she learns to trust and depend on her guide dog.

When I was eight, I went on a third-grade field trip to Guide Dogs for the Blind School in San Rafael, California. The instructors there explained how they trained the guide dogs, showing us puppies as well as dogs that had graduated from the program. They were cute, but mostly I was impressed by their intelligence. They were all eager to help the blind people with whom they were paired. When I turned sixteen, I decided I would like to get my own guide dog.

Guide Dogs for the Blind doesn't usually accept high school students into its program. So, after I had been interviewed and my cane skills had been tested, I waited nervously for three weeks. Finally, the school called and said my application had been approved, and I could enroll in the summer. I was to live there for a month and train with a dog.

 1 What problem did Tiffany hope the guide dog would solve?

For the first three days, our class worked with the instructors, learning the commands, the hand gestures, and the correct way to hold the harness. The instructors observed our walking pace and held interviews with us so they could best match us with a dog. Those three days seemed like an eternity as I wondered about my dog—what her name would be, what breed she'd be, and what her personality would be like. When the time came, I waited impatiently for my name to be called.

"Tiffany."

I jumped.

"You will be receiving Dorsey, a yellow Labrador/golden retriever crossbreed. She was born October 9th of 1995. . . ."

Dorsey? Dorsey. I tested the name softly with my tongue. I liked it. It wasn't generic, but it wasn't bizarre either. Besides, it sounded classy to have a dog named after a Big Band leader.

A few minutes later, I was led into a room where I met Dorsey for the first time. She gave me a hello kiss and then looked up as if to say, "Okay. I'm ready to go back to the kennel and see my friends." There was no bolt of lightning, no clap of thunder, no love at first lick. In fact, our friendship remained casual for the month we trained at the school. Even after we went home, the bonding didn't happen all at once. I never woke up one morning with the feeling that Dorsey and I were inseparable, but, somehow, it happened. Every day when I groom her, play with her, give her food, and have a good workout, we bond a little more.

2   What problem was Tiffany concerned about when she first got Dorsey, and how did she solve the problem?

Dorsey still amazes me. She stops at curbs and flights of stairs so I don't stumble. When asked, she can find the door, the steps, the escalator, or the elevator. But the thing that impresses me most is Dorsey's intelligent disobedience. That means she will disobey my commands when it's for my own safety. For example, at Guide Dogs school, we practiced traffic checks. I would tell Dorsey to cross a street even though an instructor was driving toward us in a car. Dorsey would refuse to cross because she recognized the danger. Fortunately, Dorsey and I have not been in such a scary situation since then. But I feel very safe knowing she is on the lookout.

I didn't think I had a problem with mobility before I got a guide dog. I could find my way around as well as the next person, but I didn't realize how stressful it was for me. Dorsey has blessed me with a freedom of movement. I now hold my head high instead of at the awkward angle that allows me to see out of the corners of my eyes. I can weave effortlessly through crowds, and I no longer shy away from shadows on the ground. When my friends ask if I need a ride, I can smile and say, "No, thanks. Dorsey and I are walking."

 3 How did Dorsey help to solve Tiffany's problem?

Raising Her Sights

By Jessica Arce

This selection is about a girl who accepts a puppy to train as a guide dog. Read the selection to find out what happens to the puppy she trains.

Five years ago, I attended three guide dog meetings and dog obedience classes. I received a puppy application that I filled out and sent to the Guide Dogs for the Blind School in San Rafael, California. A couple of months later, I received a letter from the school saying that my application had been approved and that I would receive a puppy at the next Fun Day.

Fun Day is a day when guide dog raisers and their dogs meet in one place and listen to talks and demonstrations from guide dog instructors. They go through an obstacle course so that the instructors can help with any problems the dog might have.

 4 What did Jessica want?

Finally, the day came to meet my puppy. Her name was Adriana. She was a tiny ball of dark, red fluff. I had no idea how much work she'd be. For the next few months, I taught Adriana that she had to go potty outside instead of all over the house and that the furniture was not her place to take a nap.

After Adriana had all her shots, I started taking her out with me so that she would get used to different sights, smells, and sounds. She especially needed to get used to such distractions as food on the floor, loud noises, and people. We went to restaurants, school and 4-H activities, shopping, out of town trips, and the fair. As another part of the training, I took her on stairs, elevators, boats, cars, buses, and trains. When she went outside, Adriana had to wear a green jacket that said, "Guide Dog Puppy in Training." Socializing gets a puppy ready for anything a blind person might encounter.

5   What problems was Jessica trying to help Adriana overcome?

Before I knew it, a year flew by, and my time with Adriana was up. She had grown to be a polite, well-behaved dog. Another letter came telling me it was time to return Adriana to the Guide Dog School, so she could begin her training in San Rafael.

When a guide dog returns to the school, it is put with other dogs in a group, and three to four instructors are assigned to each group. Adriana soon learned to stop for curbs and stairs and to avoid obstacles and distractions.

One day, a woman from the school called and said that Adriana had been pulled out of training because they wanted to use her for breeding, and that I was invited to her graduation. I was so excited that I started bouncing off the walls. After three long months of waiting, we set out for San Rafael.

The family that Adriana is now living with are "Breeder Keepers." Breeder Keepers live within a 50-mile radius of the school and agree to keep a breeder in their home.

A few months after I got back, Adriana's family wrote and said that Adriana had her first litter of puppies. I was excited because I was going to raise one of Adriana's babies. The new puppy, Sahara, made me so happy. The year with her sped by, and soon I returned her to the school. Today Sahara is a career change dog. Fifty percent of the dogs that return to the school do not graduate as working guides. A dog's career may then change from being a guide dog to being a therapy dog, or a search and rescue dog, or, of course, a wonderful family pet.

6 What problem is Jessica trying to solve by working with guide dog puppies?

Time to Write!

You just read two articles about two girls. Think about how the articles were alike. Think about how the articles were different.

• For this activity, you will compare and contrast the two articles you just read.

Prewriting

First, fill out the chart below.

	"Where She Leads, I Will Follow"	"Raising Her Sights"
Person involved		
Problem to be solved		
Solution		
Other		

Writing

Now, use another sheet of paper to compare and contrast the two articles.

65

You have been thinking along as you read. Now practice thinking along to help you answer test questions.

Read and Think

- Read each selection.
- Stop at each box and answer the question.
- Answer the questions at the end of each selection.

How does Fabiolita help Abuela?

When I was twelve, my grandmother—my Abuela— moved into our house in the city from her farm in the country. She said she was happy, but I noticed that Abuela didn't always look happy. Some days I would catch her putting down her knitting and staring out the window.

1   What are you thinking about now?

"Abuela," I said, "are you homesick for the farm?"

"No, mi Fabiolita, for sometimes I felt lonely there, and sometimes there was much hard work to do. But sometimes I miss the sun," Abuela said. "Oh, I know it's up there, but here the tall buildings hide it."

I looked out the window, trying to see with Abuela's eyes. Some of the houses were like ours, with only two stories, but other buildings were taller, with four or five floors. They were fairly close together, throwing many shadows on the ground. Compared to the country, it probably did seem to Abuela like she was surrounded by skyscrapers that blocked the sun. It was then that a bright idea popped into my head.

On Saturday I went to the neighborhood bodega. Señor Marquez, the owner, sells mostly fruit, vegetables, milk, and bread. But I thought I remembered a display rack I'd seen.

"Ah, Fabiolita! ¿Cómo está?" Señor Marquez said.

"Señor Marquez, do you sell seeds?" I asked.

"I don't have many, Fabiolita. What do you need? Peppers?"

"No, no," I said, as I slowly turned the display rack. "Here they are—just what Abuela needs!" I said.

 2   What are you thinking about now?

Soon I had planted the seeds in the dirt along the side of the house. Then I went inside and wrote in a small notebook: "Saturday, May 15: Planted sunshine seeds for Abuela."

Every day I checked on my garden, carefully recording how the seeds sprouted and grew. By June 15, I wrote in my notebook: "My ruler is only 12 inches long, and the sunshine stems are now too tall to measure!"

The plants grew taller and produced buds. Abuela was quite busy helping with the cooking and sewing. Still, I would occasionally find her looking out the window. Outside, while tending to my plants, I would strain my neck to peer upward at them. When doing that, I would also see Abuela at the window with a face that looked slightly puzzled.

At last the day that I had waited for arrived. One blazing bright morning in July, I peered out the window and began to shout, "Abuela! Abuela! They're blooming! Now you won't have to miss the sunshine!"

Abuela padded over to the window. Outside, sunflowers as big as dinner plates bloomed.

"Mi Fabiolita, this is a wonderful thing you have done for your Abuela! But you know what? I think you are sunshine itself, and I will always have sunshine with you around," Abuela said.

And outside the window, a small breeze caused the sunflowers to nod their heads in agreement.

3   What are you thinking about now?

Darken the circle for the correct answer.

1. The person telling this story is
   _____.
   (A) Abuela
   (B) Fabiolita
   (C) Señor Marquez
   (D) Mother

3. Which of these would make the best
   title for this story?
   (A) "A Trip to the Bodega"
   (B) "Abuela Moves In"
   (C) "Sunshine for Abuela"
   (D) "Growing a Garden"

2. At the bodega, Fabiolita buys
   _____.
   (A) sunflower seeds
   (B) a ruler
   (C) tomatoes
   (D) seeds to grow peppers

4. Compared to the country, the city
   seems to Abuela to be _____.
   (A) quieter
   (B) lonelier
   (C) more frightening
   (D) darker

Write your answer on the lines below.

5. Why does Fabiolita think the sunflowers will make Abuela feel better?

_____

_____

_____

_____

_____

Who wrote the note in the bottle?

Hans and Tanner walked the beach whenever they could, gathering driftwood and other interesting things that washed up on shore. Hans was convinced that pirates had landed on this coast and buried their treasure in one of the sand dunes along the bay.

"What's that?" he said one day, pointing at something half-buried in the sand.

"Just an old bottle," Tanner said.

"Maybe it's got a message in it!" Hans cried hopefully.

Tanner shook his head. "You won't ever give up," he mumbled as Hans pulled the bottle out of the sand and brushed crusted sea salt off it.

"There is, Tanner! There's a piece of yellow paper inside!"

---

1 What are you thinking about now?

"Oh, sure," Tanner grumbled, squinting at the bottle as Hans held it up to catch the light. "It's just somebody's joke, Hans," Tanner said, "so don't get excited. Miles and Robin are probably up in the dunes watching us and laughing like crazy. This is just the kind of stunt they would pull."

They pried an ancient-looking cork out of the neck of the bottle, and it crumbled into pieces. Then Tanner took a thin stick and stuck it into the middle of the curled paper inside. Slowly, he turned the stick, winding the paper around it.

"Hurry up!" Hans cried.

"No," Tanner said, "it seems really brittle. We need to be careful getting it out if we expect to read whatever is on it." It took over thirty minutes, while Hans kept grabbing unsuccessfully at the bottle.

When he finally got the note out, Tanner opened it carefully, and it began to crack in half.

"What does it say?" Hans shouted. "I bet it's from a Spanish galleon in trouble at sea!"

"Well, it's in English," Tanner said, "so the writer wasn't Spanish. The letters are funny, though." Haltingly he read:

"We are sinking and doomed after a howling storm splintered our mast and washed half of the crew away. The captain says we must make rafts of the lumber, but it will be hopeless, and we will freeze in this horrible sea. If you find this, please tell Emma Forsight of Liverpool that Humbert Loese loves her. Farewell!   November 11, 1798, aboard the Kettinger, for just a bit yet, Mate."

"Maybe they're still out there," Hans said breathlessly.

"Get real!" Tanner said, thinking he heard distant laughter and eyeing the grasses on the dunes, expecting to see Robin's and Miles' heads bobbing there.

 2 What are you thinking about now?

Hans went on for weeks, wondering aloud about the *Kettinger*. He knew that it was a clipper, that Humbert was surely a pirate, and that Emma might be waiting for him.

"It was over two hundred years ago!" Tanner almost shouted. "Or more likely, two weeks ago. Someone could just find an old bottle and write a note on old paper to roll up inside it. You are so gullible, Hans, that would you believe anything!" But he was thinking about how rotten the cork in the bottle was.

A few weeks later, Hans showed Tanner a book about old ships. He opened it to a page with a long list headed "English merchant vessels, 1775–1850." His finger trembled as he pointed to the middle of the list.

"The *Kettinger*," Tanner read slowly, "christened in 1777. Lost in the North Atlantic in the winter of 1798. Carried silks, incense, and other semi-precious cargo."

Tanner's head snapped back. "Wow!" he said.

"What shall we do?" Hans asked.

Tanner knew what Hans was thinking. "Well, we can't notify Emma, Hans! But let's take the bottle and note with your book to Mr. Huffman at the county museum. This is quite a find!"

3 What are you thinking about now?

Darken the circle for the correct answer.

6. In Tanner's opinion, Hans is a

   _____.

   Ⓐ historian

   Ⓑ sailor

   Ⓒ dreamer

   Ⓓ jokester

7. What suggests that the note and bottle are genuine?

   Ⓐ Miles and Robin are watching from a distance.

   Ⓑ Hans finds the ship's name in a book.

   Ⓒ Mr. Huffman wants them for his museum.

   Ⓓ The boys see the *Kettinger* in a port.

8. You can tell from the selection that the word gullible means _____.

   Ⓐ hungry for seafood

   Ⓑ frightened by water

   Ⓒ willing to believe most things

   Ⓓ careful to do research

9. Humbert wrote the note to

   _____.

   Ⓐ say goodbye

   Ⓑ seek help

   Ⓒ play a joke

   Ⓓ fool Emma

Write your answer on the lines below.

10. How are Hans and Tanner different?

   _____

   _____

   _____

   _____

   _____

   _____

How are people helping the Eastern Bluebird?

Eastern Bluebirds are well known for their beautiful feathers and lovely song. They have bright blue wings and backs that glow in the sunshine. Their orange breasts puff up when they sing. They are also one of the few birds that likes humans.

Bluebirds live in grassy areas with trees. They especially like meadows and large mowed areas, such as parks, cemeteries, yards, and golf courses. In the summer, these areas attract many insects that bluebirds eat. Grasshoppers, caterpillars, and beetles are among their favorites. In the winter, bluebirds eat many kinds of wild berries.

 1   What are you thinking about now?

Although bluebirds are not now in danger of becoming extinct, they were in danger a few years ago. People had cut down so many trees that bluebirds had trouble finding nesting places. Bluebirds nest in holes in trees, such as those made by woodpeckers. Without enough nesting places, many bluebirds did not lay eggs or raise young.

Other birds have made matters even worse. The Eastern Bluebird is a native of North America. That means that the bluebird has lived here thousands of years. However, people have brought many non-native birds to America, such as the House Sparrow and the European Starling. These birds sometimes build their nests on top of bluebird eggs, or kill baby and adult bluebirds. The sparrow and starling also eat wild berries. This makes it difficult for Eastern Bluebirds to find enough food in the winter.

In the late 1970s, people across the country began helping bluebirds. They began building thousands of nesting boxes in which Eastern Bluebirds could lay their eggs. These nesting boxes are attached to the tops of smooth, round poles. Some people put the nesting boxes in their backyards or on fence posts in the country. When many of these boxes are near each other, they are called "bluebird trails."

 2 What are you thinking about now?

People have to monitor, or frequently check, these nesting boxes for signs of danger. If sparrows or starlings have moved into a box, their nests and eggs must be taken out quickly. People who monitor bluebird nesting boxes also have to help protect the bluebirds from animals that may eat them. Cats, snakes, and raccoons all attack and eat bluebirds.

It is not hard to help protect bluebirds because they like people. If a baby bluebird falls out of its nest or a nesting box needs to be cleaned, it is fine for a person to gently pick up the bluebird. Many other birds are so afraid of humans that they will abandon any babies that people have touched.

The effort to protect the Eastern Bluebird has made a big difference. Today there are thousands more Eastern Bluebirds than there were thirty years ago. Instead of being only a memory, this beautiful songbird is becoming more common all over the eastern United States.

 3 What are you thinking about now?

Darken the circle for the correct answer.

11. Eastern Bluebirds were in danger because they were _____.
- Ⓐ eating poisonous berries
- Ⓑ unable to find enough nesting places
- Ⓒ protecting their nests
- Ⓓ being shipped to England

12. In this selection, the word <u>monitor</u> means to _____.
- Ⓐ protect
- Ⓑ take a picture of
- Ⓒ remove and clean
- Ⓓ frequently check

13. One reason that Eastern Bluebirds are not extinct is that they _____.
- Ⓐ can protect their nests from other birds
- Ⓑ are so afraid of humans
- Ⓒ can build their nests anywhere
- Ⓓ have been helped by people

14. People have most helped the Eastern Bluebird by _____.
- Ⓐ building and monitoring nesting boxes
- Ⓑ killing all its enemies
- Ⓒ taming it and keeping it indoors
- Ⓓ cutting down trees

Write your answer on the lines below.
15. Why did the Eastern Bluebird need help?

_____

_____

_____

_____

_____

Thinking About

Author's Style and Technique

Read the two advertisements below. As you read, notice the differences in the authors' styles.

NEED A GREAT JOB?

Now hiring energetic people who enjoy a fast-paced & exciting atmosphere! Full & part-time positions available. Shifts available, 5 AM to 1 PM & 5 PM to close. We pay weekly. Starting pay $6.50/hr! Benefits include free meals & uniforms! End of year bonus!

Apply in person at DAVE'S DINER.

Rusty's Restaurant

We have both full-time and part-time positions available at Rusty's Restaurant. If you want to work here, you need to be able to work under stress. One of our shifts starts early in the morning at 5 o'clock and doesn't end until 1 o'clock in the afternoon. The other shift starts at 5 o'clock in the evening and doesn't end until we close at 1 o'clock in the morning. We can only pay you $6.50 when you first start. You'll get paid every week. If you decide to work here, we'll let you eat here for free and we won't make you buy your uniform. If you work here at least a year, we'll give you a bonus. If you want to apply, you need to come to the restaurant. Don't call us.

Think about the two authors' styles. Answer the questions below.

Even authors of ads need to think about their technique.

Which advertisement appealed to you more? Why?

_____

_____

Why did the style of the other advertisement make it less appealing?

_____

_____

What else did you think of while you read the two advertisements?

_____

_____

_____

_____

Read and Think

- Read the selections that follow.
- Stop at each box and answer the question.
- Remember to think about the author's style and technique as you read.

THE STORY OF SITTING BULL, GREAT SIOUX CHIEF

by Lisa Eisenberg

Let's Read

This selection tells of the childhood of Sitting Bull. Sitting Bull was an important and famous chief of a Sioux tribe during the late 1800s. (As a child, Sitting Bull had a different name.) This selection is the first chapter of a book that tells the story of Sitting Bull's life.

The water of the Grand River was icy cold. The winter sky was a grim, stony gray. But inside the cone-shaped, buffalo-hide tipi on the south bank of the river, the air was warm. A young Sioux woman had just given birth to a baby boy, and her heart was filled with joy.

The new mother's name was Mixed Day. Beside her, an older woman was hard at work. First, she placed the tiny infant on a clean square of deerskin. Then she gently cut the umbilical cord that attached the baby to its mother. She dusted the baby's navel with a fungus powder to protect it, and tied a narrow strip of deerskin around his little stomach. After that, she cleaned the baby with warm, moist sweet grass, rubbed him down with buffalo fat, and wrapped him in blankets.

Once the baby was laid beside his mother, the older woman went to spread the news of his birth. "You have a new baby," she told a warrior who was anxiously waiting outside the tipi. "It is a son."

The new father smiled and shouted with joy. Like other Plains Indians, he believed the old saying: A man's most valuable possessions were not his horses, tipis, or weapons—they were his children. And a baby boy was to be prized above all other gifts from Wakan Tanka, the Great Spirit.

 1 What effect does the author's use of descriptive details have on the story?

Because the Lakota calendar is different from the Euroamerican people's, no one can be sure of the exact date of Sitting Bull's birth. It was probably in March, 1830 or 1831. The Sioux called that time the Winter When Yellow Eyes Played in the Snow. Sitting Bull's birthplace was in the part of the United States we now call South Dakota.

The new baby's father was a great warrior, named Returns-Again because he was always ready to return to battle. He and his wife, who would later change her name to Her Holy Door, were Hunkpapa Lakota Indians. The Hunkpapas were Tetons, which is the name given to the western division within the Great Sioux nation.

"Hunkpapa" means "Those Who Camp by the Entrance." The Hunkpapas and other Sioux tribes were hunters who lived by following buffalo herds back and forth across the Great Plains. Mighty warriors who were fiercely proud of their free and independent life, they were feared and respected by the other Plains Indians.

2 How does the author let the reader know how she feels about the Sioux?

After the birth of her son, Mixed Day rested for a few days. Then she attended a feast held in her baby's honor. The baby was cuddled and admired, but never permitted to cry. Whenever he opened his mouth to wail, Mixed Day would gently pinch his nostrils together to stop any noise. Allowing a baby to scream was just too dangerous—the noise could easily attract enemies who might attack the camp.

When the baby was about two months old, Mixed Day
started carrying him around on her back in a blanket
attached to a wooden frame called a cradleboard. When
Mixed Day was busy cooking or sewing, she often leaned the
cradleboard up against a tipi post so her young son could
watch her work. When the tribe was on the move, she hung
the cradleboard over her pony's saddlehorn, and the baby
rode there alongside cooking pots, sacks of herbs, and other
bundles.

On winter nights the baby was bundled up inside warm,
woolly buffalo robes. Often, his mother put him to bed with
his moccasins on. If an enemy attacked during the night, she
might have to grab up her children and run away from the
tent at a moment's notice.

Returns-Again and Mixed Day did not name their new baby right away; they waited to choose a name that suited his personality. In the first few months of his life, they saw nothing amazing about their son. What they did notice was that the little boy couldn't be hurried. When his mother handed him a juicy piece of food from the fire, he didn't stuff it into his mouth the way other babies did. Instead he studied it for a long time before deciding it was all right to eat. Finally the baby's parents agreed on a name for him. He would be called Hunkesni—a Sioux word that means "slow."

 3 How does the author describe the way that the Sioux named their babies?

As Slow got bigger, he was taken out of his cradleboard from time to time to practice walking. His father and the other men of the tribe were often off hunting buffalo or raiding horses from other tribes, so the little boy spent most of his time with his mother and the other women and children. As he toddled around among the cooking pots and tipis, his older sisters cuddled him and teased him. The old people of the tribe cheered his attempts at walking, telling Slow that one day he would be a great and powerful hunter and warrior.

Mixed Day and Returns-Again doted on Slow and their other children. Besides his parents, many relatives also helped take care of the little boy. If he started to cry, somebody was always around to give him what he wanted or rock him until he was happy again. No one ever told Slow "no" or gave him a spanking. If he did something wrong, somebody simply asked him to stop. That was the way all Sioux treated children.

4   How does the author let the reader know what the Sioux thought was important in raising their children?

As Slow grew older, he became too big for his cradleboard. When the Hunkpapas went on long trips, he now rode in a basket hung under the tail of Mixed Day's pony. By the time he was five years old, Slow rode behind his mother on her pony's back. A few years later, he was given his own pony.

Slow played many different games with the other children in the camp. He rode, wrestled, swam, and ran races. The boys played right along with the girls of the tribe in some games, like the Packing Game. For this, parents made small-scale tipis, *travois* (which are sledges on two poles dragged along the ground by a horse or dog), and bows and arrows for the children to play with. Slow and the other boys and girls pretended to make and break camp, and to cook and hunt, just like the adults. Even though they were having fun, they were also practicing skills they would need when they grew up.

During the winter Slow and his sisters amused themselves with wooden tops that they spun on ice, or they rode down the snowy hills on sleds made of buffalo ribs. When the weather warmed up again, and the snow melted, they often had mudball fights or made blowguns out of hollowed-out wooden stems.

By the time Slow was about nine or ten, he no longer played with his sisters or the other girls, who were now busy learning skills from their mothers and grandmothers. The girls and women of the tribe were responsible for gathering dried buffalo dung, or chips, that they used for their fires. They also had to carry water, prepare buffalo hides for their many uses, sew, cook, hunt for wild turnips and berries, and air the tipis.

5 How does the author help the reader to imagine what it would have been like to be a Sioux child?

Slow and the other boys, in contrast, began learning to hunt. Slow's father, Returns-Again, took him out into the forest and showed him the best type of wood to use for a bow. Slow learned how to cut the wood to the proper size, to smooth it on a rock, and to shape it over a fire. When the bow was polished, Slow decorated it with paint and colored horsehair. When his weapon was ready, Slow felt very proud. Again and again, he went out into the forest to practice shooting arrows from his bow. He could hardly wait until he was old enough to join a real hunting party!

But Slow and other boys still played games. One of their favorites was pretending to make a raid on a neighboring camp. Apart from the Sioux, there were many different tribes among the Plains Indians: the Cheyennes, the Crows, the Shoshones, the Snakes, the Arapahos, and many others.

Warfare between them was part of their life. Stealing and raiding were accepted as the best way to get new horses. Certain tribes, such as the Crows and the Assiniboins, had almost always been enemies with the Hunkpapas and other Sioux tribes. When Slow and his friends played their raiding games, they pretended they were conquering their parents' oldest foes.

In the summer Slow's family and the other Hunkpapas were almost always on the move, following the great herds of buffalo that roamed the plains. When scouts brought news that a new herd had been spotted, the crier, a respected older man, would ride around the circle of tipis shouting:

Many buffalo, I hear, Many buffalo, I hear,
They are coming now, They are coming now,
Sharpen your arrows, Sharpen your knives!

6   Why do you think the author chose to tell the exact words of the crier instead of summarizing for the reader what he said?

Everyone became very excited. Slow's mother and the other women would race to take down the tipis, pack up their belongings, and tie all the bundles onto the *travois*. Slow was always amazed at how quickly Mixed Day did her work. But everything the family owned was easy to move: Buffalo-hide tipis and bags made of skin could be rolled up into small, lightweight bundles. Instead of heavy pottery dishes for cooking, the Hunkpapas used buffalo pouches, which weighed very little. In fact, they owned nothing that couldn't be carried by a person, dog, or horse.

While his mother and the other women worked, Slow would jump on his pony and help herd his family's animals. Finally, everyone was assembled in a long line, ready to move. The scouts started out first, to keep watch on the buffalo. A few miles behind them rode the most important members of the tribe—the men who had "medicine," or spiritual power, and who could communicate with the Great Spirit. They carried sacred objects to help make the hunt successful. Behind them came the chiefs dressed in feathered and beaded regalia. Finally came the women, children, and old people, and the animals carrying their belongings.

As Slow trotted along beside his family, he had eyes only for the warriors, who rode on both sides of the long column to protect everyone. Warriors had the most high-spirited and fastest horses, and they looked so exciting in their face paint and eagle plumes. As Slow listened to the men chanting their bold fighting songs, his heart ached with longing.

One day, he vowed, he would become the most fearless warrior of all!

7 Why do you think that the author included this last line as its own paragraph and ended it with an exclamation mark?

Time to Write!

Imagine that you are a member of Sitting Bull's tribe. It is time for you to choose a name for yourself. What name would you choose? Why?

• For this activity, you will write an essay explaining and defending your name choice.

Prewriting

First, answer the questions below.

What are some things you do well?

_____

_____

What are some of your favorite things about yourself?

_____

_____

Choose a few of your talents or favorite things about yourself from the lists above and create a list of possible Indian names for yourself.

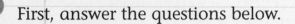

_____

_____

_____

Writing

Choose your favorite Indian name from the list you created above. On another sheet of paper, write your reasons explaining your choice.

Richard Byrd

By Melissa Stone

This selection is about a famous adventurer named Richard Byrd who began to explore Antarctica in 1928. Read the selection to learn how he survived the winter he spent alone in Antarctica in 1934.

"You should be heading back to the permanent base at Little America. Your work here at Bolling Advance Weather Base is done," said Richard Byrd in 1934.

He spoke to team members who had set up this base camp 120 miles south of the previously established coastal camp. "I'm disappointed that we didn't reach the South Pole and that we weren't able to transport enough supplies for two more people to stay here. But I'll be fine alone. One person can manage all the scientific instruments and collect the necessary data. You need to get back before the constant darkness of the Antarctic winter sets in. It's already March 28. The winter will begin soon."

"You have plenty of supplies, at least," said Pete Demas, the leader of the tractor transport. He surveyed the two long supply tunnels filled with food, books, and emergency provisions.

"I won't run out of anything," replied Byrd. He looked around the tiny wooden shack that would be his home for the Antarctic winter. "And it won't be hard to find things in here. When you've only got a space nine feet by thirteen feet to move around in, everything stays pretty handy. Thanks for getting all this ready! I know it was a hard job chiseling this pit out of eight feet of ice in temperatures of 50 degrees below zero."

 1 Why do you think the author used dialogue to convey so much important background information?

"You're the one that will have the hard job—staying here alone all winter," said Demas. "Remember to make sure that the stove is venting properly. Otherwise, the fumes from the burning kerosene could be dangerous. Be sure to check that all the fumes are going outside."

"Don't worry," Byrd replied. "I'll check the venting pipes every couple of days to make sure they're working."

"I sure don't like to leave you here all alone." Demas shifted uncomfortably from foot to foot. "What if you get sick or injured?"

"I'll be fine," Byrd replied confidently. He had faith in his ability to handle any emergency. In fact, he was excited about the months that lay ahead. Then, locking eyes with Demas, Byrd gave one final order.

"No matter what happens, I'm giving a hard-and-fast order not to come for me until the winter is over. In a few weeks it will be dark 24 hours a day. Frigid temperatures, blizzards, and hidden crevasses will make travel treacherous. It will simply be too risky. Is that understood?"

Demas and the other crew members nodded somberly. One by one, they shook Byrd's hand. Then the group departed. Byrd watched until they faded into the horizon. He knew it was the last sign of life he would see for many months.

 2 How does the author let the reader know about the dangers of the Antarctic winter?

During his first few days alone, Byrd established a daily routine. In the morning, he took outside weather readings, ate breakfast, and did stretching exercises. Then he cleaned and adjusted all the weather instruments. After lunch came more measurements and observations, then a walk. Every Sunday, Tuesday, and Thursday he had lengthy radio conversations with the men back at Little America. He reported the weather data he had collected and took care of other business. In the evening he took a sponge bath, made more measurements, and cooked dinner. Then he played cards and read one of the books he had brought with him.

"It sounds like a calm, peaceful schedule," he thought. "But the reality is not that easy."

Indeed it was not. His oil stove died out every night, so the morning temperature of the shack was often 40 degrees below zero. Byrd had to climb into clothes that were frozen stiff. The kerosene he used to light his lantern was as thick as molasses from the cold. If he touched the frozen metal of the lamp, his skin stuck to it. He had to chop and melt ice for drinking water. If he let his cup of water sit for a minute, it would freeze over before he could drink it.

Outside, temperatures ranged from about plus 10 degrees to minus 75 degrees Fahrenheit. Within days his nose, cheeks, chin, and fingers were frostbitten.

On April 18, Byrd spent several hours outside, clearing a snowdrift away from the shack door. He noticed ice in the stovepipe. Although he didn't think much about it at the time, the ice was a sign that the ventilation system was not working properly. As snow blew into the venting pipes, it melted. Then, when the stove died down, the melted snow froze solid. As ice built up in the pipes, fumes from the stove were forced back into the tiny shack. Although Byrd cleaned out the pipes every few days, that was not enough. The pipe seams inside the cabin were also leaking. Slowly, ever so slowly, he was being poisoned by carbon monoxide.

 3 How does the author help you imagine what it would be like to be Richard Byrd?

A couple of weeks later, Byrd experienced his first real problem from the fumes. At the end of the day he felt anxious and depressed.

"What is wrong with me?" he puzzled. "Why am I feeling so terrible?"

He could not think of a suitable reason. After all, his day had been quiet and productive. But as he sat writing in his journal, he felt a dull ache behind his eyes and a constant pounding in his head.

A thought crossed his mind. "Maybe the fumes from the stove are bothering me. I am certainly tired of the oily smell in the air." But, he concluded in his journal, "The most likely explanation is that the trouble lies with myself."

"Yes," he thought, laying down his journal, "I must be suffering from loneliness and depression. I can't allow myself to give in to solitude. I've got to be tough if I'm going to last all winter."

4 How would this passage be different if the author had told about how Byrd felt rather than providing the reader with his thoughts?

Although he didn't want to admit it, Byrd was becoming physically sick. Even when he was out in the open air, he felt weak and nauseated. Then, on May 31, after 70 days at Advance Base, Richard Byrd collapsed.

For hours he lay on the frozen floor of his shack. At last, however, a dim consciousness returned. He felt shooting pains in his head, his stomach, his eyes. He tried to move, but found that his hands and feet were numb. Through the haze in his mind, he realized that he had all the symptoms of carbon monoxide poisoning. He managed to turn the stove off and crawl into his sleeping bag. For the next three days he lay there, hovering near death. His body throbbed with pain. Although he was terribly thirsty, he was so weak that he could barely get out of bed and melt ice to drink. Every movement required excruciating effort. If the carbon monoxide poisoning did not kill him, the cold or starvation probably would.

Finally, on June 3, a thought floated to the surface of Byrd's hazy brain.

"Today is Sunday," he realized. "The crew at Little America will be trying to reach me on the radio."

Although he knew he was in trouble, he did not want anyone at the coastal base to find out.

"They might attempt a rescue mission," he thought. "And that I can't allow."

 5 How do you think the author feels about Richard Byrd?

Byrd summoned his strength. He crawled out of his sleeping bag, cleaned the ice out of the stovepipe, reinstalled it, and lit the stove. As heat began to fill the shack, he made his way to the radio. There he struggled to send out a clear message. After signing off, he fell back onto his bunk, exhausted. The effort had sapped all his strength.

"I've got to stay alive," he whispered to himself. "If I stop sending messages, they'll know something is wrong, and they'll come for me!"

With every ounce of energy he had left, Byrd began his fight for survival. He remained incredibly weak. It required an iron will to force himself to do the basic things. He trained himself to move slowly and do just the most essential tasks. He kept the stove lit only during the coldest times so he wouldn't freeze. He took weather readings and sent them back to Little America. And he cooked meals even though he had to force himself to eat. It was a tremendous struggle.

Slowly, with agonizing sameness, June and July passed. Some days Byrd could barely make it out of bed. On his best days he only functioned at half-speed. He was living on nothing but his will power.

"I must last until spring!" he told himself again and again. "They must not come after me now."

6 How does the author build suspense about what is going to happen to Richard Byrd?

By late June the men at Little America were becoming suspicious. They noticed something was wrong with Byrd's radio messages.

"He always sends very short messages. And half the time they don't make any sense," the radio operator said.

"As soon as possible, I think we should head out to Advance Base," Demas declared.

The men all knew it wouldn't be safe until October. But they agreed Byrd might not make it that long. When the weather cleared for a few days in early August, Demas sent a message to Byrd saying he was on his way. Then on August 4, he and two others headed toward Advance Base on a snow tractor.

The trip was extremely harrowing. At one point they almost fell into a deep, hidden crevasse. But on August 11, 1934, they arrived at Advance Base.

Richard Byrd came out to meet them. He barely resembled the commander they had left four and a half months ago. He was scarecrow thin, and his eyes had sunk into his head. His hair was long and disheveled, and his clothes were dirty. He offered them some hot soup, then collapsed to the frozen ground.

For two months they took care of him and nursed him back to health. They were amazed that he had survived at all.

"I never knew a man could endure so long on sheer will power," Demas said softly.

 7 How did the author make this selection interesting to read?

Time to Write!

You read about Richard Byrd's winter in Antarctica. Now imagine what it would have been like to be Richard Byrd during this time. Describe how you think he felt when he first realized he was sick. Include a description of the setting.

- For this activity, you will write a journal entry describing what Richard Byrd thought and felt when he first realized he was sick.

Prewriting

First, answer the questions below.

Why was Richard Byrd alone in Antarctica?

_____

_____

Where was he living in Antarctica?

_____

_____

How did Richard Byrd realize that he was sick?

_____

_____

Why didn't he want to ask for help?

_____

_____

Writing

Now, use another sheet of paper to write an entry in Richard Byrd's journal.

When Justice Failed: The Fred Korematsu Story

By Steven A. Chin

This selection is the first chapter from a book about a Japanese American man named Fred Korematsu. Fred Korematsu was imprisoned by the United States government in an internment camp during World War II. Read the selection to learn about Fred Korematsu and the treatment of Japanese Americans during World War II.

Karen Korematsu watched her friend Maya Okada nervously approach the front of the class. Their social studies teacher, Mr. Wishnoff, had asked the students to give oral reports about some aspect of World War II. Maya was to present the last report on this spring afternoon in 1967.

Sunlight streamed through the dusty venetian blinds, filling the classroom with a warm, sleepy haze. Students tried to keep their attention focused on Maya, but their eyes and minds wandered. After listening to presentations all period, they were feeling bored and restless. Some gazed idly at the large maps of the United States and the world that hung on one wall of the classroom. In another hour, school would be out, and they could enjoy the rest of this sunny day.

1 What words does the author use to help you picture the setting for this selection?

Like most of her classmates, Karen was looking forward to the end of the period. But it wasn't because she was bored. In fact, she was feeling tense as she watched Maya make her way to the front of the class. Karen didn't like talking about World War II. She and Maya were the only Japanese Americans in the class, and their classmates often made fun of them whenever the topic of World War II came up at school.

During the war, Americans had scornfully called their Japanese enemies "Japs" or "Nips" or "Tojo." Such insults were repeated in the many movies and TV shows made about the war. Classmates cruelly directed these same offensive words at Karen and Maya, as if they were enemies of the United States and not American citizens. It was hard for the girls to understand their classmates' mean behavior. All Karen and Maya knew was it made them angry, and hurt their feelings—and there was nothing they could do to stop it.

Standing in front of the class in her white blouse and freshly ironed skirt, Maya announced in a clear voice that her report would be about what happened to Japanese Americans living in the United States during World War II.

"Oh, no!" thought Karen worriedly. "Why did she pick that topic? This will only make things worse."

 2   What does the author tell you to help you picture Maya?

Maya explained that after the Japanese bombed Pearl Harbor, many Americans blamed Japanese Americans for the attack and accused them of acting as spies for the Japanese government. Life became hard for Japanese Americans, especially for those living on the Pacific Coast. People called them ugly names, mistreated them, even attacked them at times. But that was just the beginning.

Three months after the Pearl Harbor bombing, Maya continued, the United States Army ordered all Japanese Americans on the West Coast to be put into internment camps. The Army had been given the power to do this by a special order from President Franklin Roosevelt. The camps were supposed to prevent Japanese Americans from spying or trying to destroy American military property.

As Maya spoke of the internment camps, Karen listened in astonishment. She had never heard of such camps before.

The internment camps were like prisons, her friend explained. There were ten camps in all. Barbed-wire fences ran around the camps, and armed soldiers stood guard to make sure no one escaped. Japanese-American families had to live in cramped barracks as if they were prisoners of war.

Students' eyes focused on Maya as she reported that more than 112,000 Japanese Americans were imprisoned during the war. They were the only group of American citizens singled out in this way, she said. Even though the United States also went to war against Germany and Italy, President Roosevelt did not allow German Americans or Italian Americans to be forced into internment camps.

Several Japanese Americans refused to obey President Roosevelt's order to report to the camps, Maya went on, including a man from California named Korematsu. Korematsu believed the government had no right to force him from his home because of his Japanese heritage. He took his case against Roosevelt's order all the way to the Supreme Court.

 3 Why do you think the author tells so much information through Maya's school report instead of telling it directly?

Karen gasped when she first heard her family name. "It couldn't be my father," she thought, "not in a million years. Maybe it's one of my uncles."

Then she heard Maya actually say her father's name: "Fred Korematsu." Karen could feel all 34 students in the classroom staring at her, waiting for her to explain the connection between herself and the man. "Is that your father? Is that your father?" everyone, including Mr. Wishnoff, seemed to be asking at once.

Karen didn't know how to respond. She honestly didn't know whether the man was her father or not. What if it was her father? Why would he keep this a secret from her? Had he really broken the law?

Karen felt confused, angry, and embarrassed. She didn't know what to think. But she did know that she was mad at Maya for not having told her the topic of her report. How could Maya have presented all that information to the class without warning her beforehand? The remaining minutes it took Maya to finish her report seemed like an eternity to Karen.

When the bell finally rang to end the period, Karen rushed over to Maya.

"Where did you find out about this?" Karen demanded, clearly upset. "Why didn't you tell me you were going to do this?"

"I thought you already knew," Maya replied, surprised by her friend's harsh tone.

"Well, I didn't," snapped Karen. "I had no idea."

 4   What are you thinking about now?

Then Karen headed for the nearest public phone in the school. Inside the phone booth, she grabbed the receiver, jammed a nickel into the coin slot, and quickly dialed her home phone number. How on earth could her parents have kept this from her? she asked herself. *Brring . . . brring . . . brring.* She would get to the bottom of this, and fast. *Brring . . . brring.* Another ten rings and still no answer. No one was home. Karen slammed down the receiver in frustration.

The halls were empty by the time she left the phone booth. All the other students had gone off to their last classes. Still confused and upset, Karen hurried off to hers.

Throughout math class, Karen replayed Maya's report over and over in her mind. She hardly heard a word the teacher was saying. She was hurt that her parents had kept such a big secret from her. She was embarrassed that her father may have been guilty of breaking the law. She was afraid her classmates would now tease her about her father the law-breaker, the Jap spy.

Finally, the bell rang, signaling the end of the day. Karen rushed past her friends mingling in the hallway and raced out the door. She hurried home as fast as she could.

Karen's mother, Kathryn, was in the kitchen preparing dinner when she heard the front door slam.

Karen burst into the kitchen. "Who was this person who challenged the internment?" she shouted. "Was it Dad?"

Kathryn was startled by her daughter's abrupt entrance and rapid-fire questions. Like her father, Karen usually kept her thoughts to herself.

"Is it Dad?" Karen shouted again before her mother could answer.

"Yes, that was your father," said Kathryn.

"Why didn't anyone tell me this?" Karen was more upset than ever.

"Your father didn't want to talk about it," replied Kathryn gently. "It happened a long time ago and it's over."

"Well, are there any papers? Is there anything I can read about it?" Karen asked impatiently.

"Your father doesn't have any documents," answered Kathryn.

 5 How does the author help you understand how eager Karen is to find out more about her father?

Karen was frustrated by the lack of progress she was making. It would be several more hours before her father returned from work. She couldn't wait that long, so she pleaded with her mother to tell all that she knew. They sat down at the kitchen table, and Karen began asking question after question.

At first Kathryn responded haltingly, straining to remember the details of events that had happened years earlier. Kathryn had not even known Fred until the war was over. Slowly, however, she began to remember things that Fred had told her over the years, and she shared those memories with Karen.

Later on, when Fred came home, Karen pressed him to explain why he had resisted internment so many years earlier. But like many Japanese Americans of his generation, Karen's father was reluctant to talk about that part of the past.

Many years before the Pearl Harbor bombing, Japanese immigrants to the United States, including Fred Korematsu's own father, had faced many difficulties. American laws had made it illegal for them to own land or become American citizens. The only jobs they could get were those that most white people didn't want.

Decades later, after the bombing, the situation grew much worse. Fred Korematsu and thousands of other Japanese Americans lost not only their jobs, homes, and belongings, but their ideals of what America was all about as well. It was a time when Japanese Americans were stripped of their honor and betrayed by their own country. To retell the story of that time was to relive it, with all its humiliation, rage, and pain. Yet it was a story that, in the end, had to be told, not only for the sake of personal honor but also for the sake of the country.

6 Why do you think the author chose to start this book about Fred Korematsu by telling about his daughter?

Time to Write!

Imagine what Fred Korematsu told his daughter when she asked him about his past. What do you think he said when she asked him to explain why he had resisted internment?

• For this activity, you will write the story of Fred Korematsu as you think he would have told it to his daughter.

Prewriting

First, answer the questions below to help you plan your story.

What was the situation like for Fred Korematsu and other Japanese Americans before the war?

_____

_____

What was the situation like after the war started?

_____

_____

What did Fred Korematsu decide to do?

_____

Why do you think he decided to do this?

_____

_____

Writing

Now, use another sheet of paper to write the story that Fred Korematsu told his daughter Karen.

Thinking Along on Tests

You have been thinking along as you read. Now practice thinking along to help you answer test questions.

Read and Think

- Read each selection.
- Stop at each box and answer the question.
- Answer the questions at the end of each selection.

How did Mrs. Brensley figure out who gave her the pen?

Mrs. Brensley was surprised to find the beautiful little package on her desk. She did not want to encourage her students to give her gifts. Some of them could not afford to buy any. She was also afraid some might think that she would play favorites.

So she quickly and quietly slipped the gift into the center drawer of her desk while looking at the class to see who might be watching her. Only Annabel Peterson was watching and asked, "What was that, Mrs. Brensley?" On being told that it was a package, Annabel asked quite boldly, "Who for?"

"For *whom*, Annabel," Mrs. Brensley said, deciding that it was not Annabel who left the gift, for Annabel would know whom it was for if she had left it.

Once the students were busy, Mrs. Brensley quietly opened the drawer just far enough to unwrap the package inside it. It was a beautiful fountain pen, marbled in green and black. There was a note inside the package that read, "From a secret student who thinks you are super! He wrapped this package hisself."

"Oh, dear," Mrs. Brensley thought, "I may never know who left this." She did not recognize the big printing. It was not terribly important to figure it out, but it became a mystery that fascinated her.

 1   What are you thinking about now?

One-third of the 33 students in the class were off that day in another room taking special tests. Besides those 11, three more were absent. So with Annabel, that made a total of 15 who could not have been the gift-giver.

When the remaining students were busy working on projects and Mrs. Brensley moved about the room to help them, Eduardo Hidalgo whispered, "I know who gave you the gift. I saw him put it there."

"Now," Mrs. Brensley thought, "that is helpful, for of the 18 students who could still be the gift-giver, 12 are girls." Apparently it was not Eduardo, so that left 5 boys. Two of those, Zachary Switterston and Michael Arster, loved getting attention, so if one of those boys had given it, he would have wanted everyone to know. That left 3 students.

Patrick Wellsing was not very artistic and probably could never have tied the bow on the package "hisself."

Bryan Muster's grammar was perfect, and he never would have used "hisself" instead of "himself" in the note.

Sean O'Connersly was almost an expert on his home computer and probably would have printed the note on that. And, besides, he had once argued in class that expensive pens were a silly investment in the computer age.

So it did not seem to Mrs. Brensley that any of her students could have left the pen. When it came time to go home, Bryan stopped at her desk to ask about the math assignment. She suggested he write it down. He readily agreed, but he could not find his pencil.

"May I please borrow your pen, Mrs. Brensley?" he asked, leaning over her desk so he could see if she opened the center drawer.

 2   What are you thinking about now?

Bryan's little brother Kendall, who was in the first grade, had come to the door of Mrs. Brensley's room so he could ride home on the bus with Bryan. He stood waiting patiently.

"I'm not certain that I have one with ink in it," she said, handing Bryan a pencil. His face became very glum, and he lowered his chin, looking at her over his glasses.

"Sure you do!" Bryan's little brother said from the doorway. "He put ink in it hisself."

Mrs. Brensley smiled and handed Bryan the pen. His face brightened and then got very red. "Thank you," Bryan said, after he had written down the math assignment and handed back the beautiful pen.

"Thank you, Bryan," Mrs. Brensley said. Turning to Kendall, she said, "And thank you, Kendall, for your note. I'm sure that Bryan will explain to you that the correct word is 'himself,' not 'hisself'."

 3   What are you thinking about now?

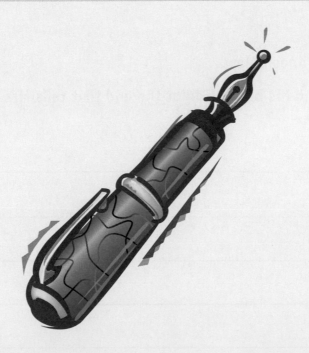

Darken the circle for the correct answer.

1. **Which of the following would make the best title for this selection?**
    (A) "Patrick Wellsing Learns to Tie a Bow"
    (B) "Why Teachers Don't Want Gifts"
    (C) "Mrs. Brensley Solves a Mystery"
    (D) "Kendall Muster's Grammar Problem"

2. **How did Mrs. Brensley know that 14 students could not have left the pen?**
    (A) They were not in class that day.
    (B) They were all boys.
    (C) They did not look at her when she put the package away.
    (D) They knew what the math assignment was for the day.

3. **Why did Bryan Muster ask to use Mrs. Brensley's pen?**
    (A) He wanted to see what the pen looked like.
    (B) He wanted her to know where it came from.
    (C) He wanted to be sure that she got it.
    (D) He did not want to write down the assignment in pencil.

4. **Who wrote the note that came with the pen?**
    (A) Bryan Muster
    (B) Annabel Peterson
    (C) Sean O'Connersly
    (D) Kendall Muster

Write your answer on the lines below.

5. **Explain what Bryan and his brother do at the end that tells Mrs. Brensley who gave her the gift.**

_____

_____

_____

_____

How did Maya Lin affect people's lives?

Many people might not know the name Maya Lin. However, she designed something that millions of Americans visit every year— the Vietnam Veterans Memorial in Washington, D.C.

Many memorials in Washington, D.C., are dedicated to famous leaders, such as presidents. Some of these memorials are tall structures made from white stone and marble. The planners of the Vietnam Veterans Memorial wanted something different to honor the Americans who fought and died in the Vietnam War.

In 1981, the planners of the memorial decided to hold a competition to find the best design. Because the memorial was so important, the planners set rules for the design. It had to be a quiet, thoughtful place. It had to blend in with the nearby lawns and memorials in Washington, D.C. It had to contain the names of all who died or remained missing in the Vietnam War. And it could make no political statement about the war.

1   What are you thinking about now?

Of the 1,400 designs, Maya Lin's was chosen as the best by every judge. Many people were surprised to learn that Maya Lin was so young. When she won the competition, she was a 21-year-old architecture student at Yale University.

Maya Lin's memorial design is unique, but simple. The memorial is made of two polished black granite walls set into the side of a hill. The walls are engraved with 57,661 names. The names are listed in order of date of death. Some people wanted the names to be in alphabetical order. However, Maya Lin thought that ordering the names by date would give each person a special place in history. "I wanted them in chronological order so that a veteran could find his time within the panel. It's like a thread of life," Lin said. The wall is also very personal for visitors because its surface is like a mirror. When people look at the names on the wall, they see an image of themselves on the wall's polished surface.

 2   What are you thinking about now?

Some groups objected to Maya Lin's design. But she insisted that the design would help people deal with their feelings about the war. "I didn't want [something] that people would just look at," she said, but "something they could relate to."

Visitors to the Vietnam Veterans Memorial react strongly to the beauty and dignity of the memorial. Many cry as they touch the names of family members and friends. Other visitors trace names on paper or leave photographs, letters, war medals, candles, and many other things that have special meaning to them. The memorial has become a place of healing. One veteran said that it is a place where "the living and dead could meet." As Maya Lin hoped, the memorial has become a gift to all Americans, not just to those who died.

3   What are you thinking about now?

Darken the circle for the correct answer.

6. Maya Lin wanted the names ordered by date of death because _____.
   Ⓐ there were so many names
   Ⓑ this is how names are usually listed on memorials
   Ⓒ it would give each person a place in history
   Ⓓ it was a requirement set by the memorial planners

7. **What aspect of the wall makes it especially unique and personal?**
   Ⓐ It is made of polished granite that reflects each visitor's image.
   Ⓑ It has a place where visitors engrave their own names.
   Ⓒ It encourages people to make political statements about the war.
   Ⓓ It is attached to a tall, white pillar.

8. Maya Lin and the memorial planners wanted the Vietnam Veterans Memorial to be _____.
   Ⓐ a place that made a lot of money
   Ⓑ a big building honoring the leaders of the war
   Ⓒ a place where children could run and play
   Ⓓ a quiet place of healing

9. Some people cry at the memorial because they are _____.
   Ⓐ disappointed with the design
   Ⓑ remembering friends and family members who have died
   Ⓒ wishing they had not come there
   Ⓓ feeling sorry for Maya Lin

Write your answer on the lines below.

10. In what ways does the Vietnam Veterans Memorial affect the people who visit it?

_____

_____

_____

_____

What is surface tension and how does it work?

Surface tension is a force that occurs at the surface of a liquid. The molecules in a liquid are held together by a force. At the surface of a liquid, this force makes the surface act like an elastic film—like a thin, strong "skin." For this reason, the film can support light objects, such as insects that regularly "walk" on water. In this project, you will perform two experiments to show the effects of surface tension.

Experiment 1

Materials
1 eyedropper
water
1 coin

Procedure
1. Use the eyedropper to slowly drop several drops of water onto a coin that is lying on a flat surface.
2. Continue to add drops one at a time. Be sure not to touch the coin or the water on it with the dropper.
3. Keep adding drops until a dome of water forms on the surface of the coin. How many drops can you add until the water rolls off?

 1 What are you thinking about now?

Experiment 2

Materials

water
1 plastic cup
2 paper clips

Procedure

1. Place a nearly full cup of water on a flat surface. Make sure the surface is stable and does not shake.
2. Bend a paper clip at a right angle and use it carefully to lower another paper clip onto the surface of the water.
3. If it does not float, keep trying. Try not to upset the water's surface.

DRAWING CONCLUSIONS

What did each of the experiments show about surface tension? Using the information provided in the introduction, can you explain why the experiments worked?

EXTENSION

To observe how to break surface tension, add one drop of dishwashing liquid to the water dome in Experiment 1 or to the glass with the floating paper clip in Experiment 2.

2   What are you thinking about now?

Darken the circle for the correct answer.

11. Both of these experiments show the force of _____.
  Ⓐ liquid
  Ⓑ surface tension
  Ⓒ elastic film
  Ⓓ paper clips

12. In Experiment 1, why do the instructions say, "Be sure not to touch the coin or the water on it with the dropper"?
  Ⓐ Because the dropper wouldn't work.
  Ⓑ Because the coin would be too slippery.
  Ⓒ Because the water would begin to roll off.
  Ⓓ Because the paper clip would sink.

13. In Experiment 2, why should you make sure the flat surface is stable and does not shake?
  Ⓐ So the water in the cup will be still and smooth.
  Ⓑ So you can bend the paper clip more easily.
  Ⓒ So the plastic cup doesn't turn over.
  Ⓓ So the coin won't sink.

14. What makes the paper clip float on the water?
  Ⓐ an insect
  Ⓑ an eyedropper
  Ⓒ dishwashing liquid
  Ⓓ surface tension

Write your answer on the lines below.

15. Which of the two experiments do you think would be harder to do? Why?

_____

_____

_____

_____

_____

_____

Acknowledgments

Grateful acknowledgment is made to the following authors and publishers for the use of copyrighted materials. Every effort has been made to obtain permission to use previously published material. Any errors or omissions are unintentional.

"The Kicking Cow" by Barbara Bartholomew. Reprinted by permission of CRICKET magazine, April 1993, Vol. 20, No. 8, © 1993 by Barbara Bartholomew.

Reprinted from *Morning Girl* by Michael Dorris. Chapter 7, "Morning Girl." Copyright © 1992 by Michael Dorris. Published by Hyperion Books for Children.

"Raising Her Sights" by Jessica Arce. Reprinted, with permission, from *New Moon*®: *The Magazine for Girls and Their Dreams*. Copyright New Moon Publishing, Duluth, Minnesota.

"Richard Byrd" by Melissa Stone. In *Flying High*, copyright © 1989 Steck-Vaughn Company.

"Seed Travel" by Ann Ackroyd. Reprinted by permission of SPIDER magazine, June 1998, Vol. 5, No. 6, © 1998 by Ann Ackroyd.

From *The Story of Sitting Bull, Great Sioux Chief* by Lisa Eisenberg. Chapter 1, "A Baby Named Slow." Copyright © 1991 by Parachute Press. Used by permission of Dell Publishing, a division of Random House, Inc.

From *Walking the Road to Freedom: A Story About Sojourner Truth* by Jeri Ferris. Copyright © 1988 by Carolrhoda Books, Inc. Used by permission of the publisher. All rights reserved.

When Justice Failed: The Fred Korematsu Story by Steven A. Chin. Chapter 1, "The Report." Copyright © 1993 by Dialogue Systems, Inc. Published by Steck-Vaughn Company.

"Where She Leads, I Will Follow" by Tiffany Medina. Reprinted, with permission, from *New Moon*®: *The Magazine for Girls and Their Dreams*. Copyright New Moon Publishing, Duluth, Minnesota.

From "The Wise Old Woman" adapted by Yoshiko Uchida. In *The Sea of Gold and Other Tales from Japan*, published by Charles Scribner's Sons, 1965. Courtesy of the Bancroft Library, University of California, Berkley.

Illustration Credits

Cindy Salans Rosenheim, pp. 4, 40, 78; Corinne Okada Takara, cover, pp. 6–16; Clint Hansen, pp. 18–26; Gwen Connelly, cover, pp. 29–38; Glory Bechtold, pp. 42–46; John Dyess, cover, pp. 48–56; Michael Dean, pp. 66, 68, 70, 72, 116, 119; Bruce Bowles, cover, pp. 80–90; Ron Himler, pp. 92–102; Todd Leonardo, cover, pp. 105–113; Andromeda Oxford Ltd., pp. 125–126.

Photography Credits

Cover Sam Dudgeon; pp. 5, 41 Rick Williams; pp. 58, 61 Courtesy Tiffany Medina; p. 62 ©PhotoDisc; p. 64 ©Richard Sobol/Animals Animals; p. 74 ©S. Michael Bisceglie/Animals Animals; p. 76 ©Richard Day/Animals Animals; p. 79 Rick Williams; pp. 81, 82, 84, 87, 88 (backgrounds) CORBIS/©Werner Forman; p. 107 CORBIS; p. 114 Culver Pictures; p. 121 CORBIS/Bettmann; p. 123 Reuters/Win McNamee/Archive Photos.